PERPETUAL MOTION GENIUS' GUIDE TO WRITING

Nathan Coppedge

PERPETUAL MOTION

GENIUS' GUIDE TO

WRITING

Nathan Coppedge

INTRODUCTION

Nathan Coppedge

I have developed a rigorous writing method over the course of the years. I have benefited from such texts as Natalie Goldberg's *Writing Down the Bones*, Annie Dillard's *A Writing Life*, and Ann LaMott's *Bird by Bird* --- and even Stephen King's notorious *How to Write*. In the process of reading these books, I have come to a number of profound conclusions concerning the art of writing --- which mostly serve as practical suggestions for the 'writing seeker'. One of these concerns the importance of the title of a work, and others relate to the specifically existential craft of producing writing. This text includes my best tips on writing, tips I have already used to influence nascient writers on the web.

Nathan Coppedge

GUIDE TO WRITING

Nathan Coppedge

1. Original Writing

Originality is not difficult. Originally-eventually, every person's writing would have a kind of holiness. In some ways holiness is the only natural kind of writing. In my view it is holiness, not acceptability, which makes a work original. After all, fashion is merely democracy, and is not always circumspect. Editors are bound to consider democracy as a virtue, when it may not be ultimately.

2. Quantity

For most people, it is quantity that is difficult. For other people, it is authenticity. Following the quantity paradigm, most people are led to the terrain in which stimulation is the available option, because productivity is the paradigm. This is unfortunate. Stimulation is not a good option for people who have trouble with authenticity, either.

3. Editing

An original writer can edit by con-
sidering what is on his or her
mind. By contrast, someone who
must consider others' opinions is
bound to be confused and make a
mistaken judgment. Therefore,
there is no option but to consider
what is original in the original
sense when making editing cor-
rections. Otherwise, stimulation is
all that is being shown in the writing. That is a recipe for disaster.

4. The Big Picture: Your Title

The biggest mistake anyone may make is to avoid the big picture. One major reason for this is that the big picture is what figures most prominently into your choice of a title for the book. If the title doesn't work, it turns out, your book is unmarketable. So the big picture counts for a lot. In this sense, every writer is a philosopher.

5. A First Approach: Poetic Writing

Of course, many writers would have you believe that their work is poetic. Poetry is what seems beautiful. But, it turns out, poetry slows writing way down. It may be simpler to get to the point, to tell a story, or to make a list of things that seem interesting. More often than not, a successful writer at some point turns to non-fiction.

6. A Second Approach: Hodge-Podge

Lists and books of quotations are not always suitable for publication. But that does not mean it is impossible. It's a matter of having something that is suitable for an audience, something arranged neatly enough or with enough complexity to have popular appeal. An encyclopedia is an example of this. An encyclopedia can begin as a bulleted list, and expand creatively.

7. A Third Approach: Organization

Using chapters is a simple way to expand the potential of a fiction work. The same goes for non-fiction: dividing into numbered sections and sub-sections grants much additional potential to your work. You have a choice: either expand each section to be very large, or opt for writing a shorter work. Another option is committing a lot of time to writing it.

Nathan Coppedge

8. A Fourth Approach: Perfection-ism.

Often at some point within the previous methods a writer will find their own impulse towards perfectionism. Perfectionism is the beginning of writing serious work. It requires developing elaborate methods to improve, hone, and re-embellish materials that are otherwise worthless. Typically, you have a choice here between originality and informa-tion.

9. Factors

Factors like an obsession with math, an interesting personality, or a love for the sound of sentences can go a long way towards establishing the core of a book before it is even finished being written. For those less fortunate, it may help to coerce these abilities---a love of semantics, an interest in gardening, etc.---to emerge artificially, purely for the sake of the writing.

10. Productivity

Remember, not much writing is necessary to write a book in a year. In a 6" X 9" format, you only need a page every two or three days to write over 100 pages, even with editing. Consider plan-ning to write a longer book every now and then, and shorter books when you feel inspired.

11. Inspiration

When you have free time and you're not being productive, go out and see the world, and per- haps take some loose-leaf paper with you. Use these small inklings of ideas to found the beginnings of future projects. When you feel like it, you can expand on these ideas in a more extended form, sometimes using lists or outside- source quotes.

12. Joie d' Vivre

Remember not to lose the only you you have---yourself. It would be a disaster to think that writing is more important than who you are as a person. Even if you have no personality and live in a garage, writing is a reflection of you, and writing depends on you. You are more important than what you write about, necessarily. You are also responsible personally for everything you write.

13. Choosing Subject-Matter

Oftentimes the first major hurdle to writing occurs when the void opens up, and one cannot think of a topic to write about. Oftentimes the answer is that what one should write is something more specific or more general than anticipated. Then you have to make up your mind not to disappoint anybody.

14. Being Popular

Popularity is about being an expert. Whether the expertise is revealed or else concealed, in some way how expert you are determines how much you appeal to an audience, which in turn influences how popular you are. Another factor is marketing, which requires shrewd business decisions.

15. Sustained Writing

Writing over long periods of time may drain energy. Watch your personal habits and make sure nothing else is the real culprit. Also be sure about other things: (A) Are you writing what you care to write about? And, (B) Are you writing with your professional interest in mind? Answering these questions can help to steer your path into greater productivity.

16. Groping in the Dark

Some of the greatest insights occur while we are immersed in the
assumption of stupidity. Inspiration can occur easily even without
a feeling of inspiration. An inspired idea is just an inspired
idea. It is nothing impossible or
grandiose, necessarily. Monitoring
our sensations can give us para-
doxical inklings of something far
greater than what we originally
set out to produce.

17. Worse Comes to Worst

Keep your options open as much as possible. You may be a fringe-thinking historical writer, or a stupidly popular novelist, or you may be some combination of these, or something entirely different. Each of these options is treated differently by the media. Who you are is not always what you appear to become.

18. Immortality

Of course, everything depends on who you are as a person. There are many types of gifts in this universe. All you need is one kind of fame, one kind of fortune, one kind of promise, one kind of desire, etc. One thing is enough to succeed, as long as it's not too simple. Be who you are is the key to knowing how to succeed. You too can have relative immortality. All you need to do is know how to succeed.

THE END OF THIS TEXT

Nathan Coppedge

OTHER BOOKS IN THE PERPETUAL MOTION GENIUS' GUIDE SERIES

Guide for Intelligent Babies
Guide for Intelligent Children
Guide for Inteligent Y. Adults
Guide for Inteligent Y. Poets
Guide to Arch. & Autos.
Guide to Historic Deaths
Guide to Interface Design
Guide to Meaning
Guide to Philosophy

OTHER POPULAR TITLES

Nathan Coppedge's Perpetual
   Motion Machine Designs &
   Theory
The Dimensional Philoso-
   pher's Toolkit
How to Write Aphorisms
The Scientific Papers

BIO

Nathan Coppedge is the author of numerous books, including other editions of the Perpetual Motion Genius' Guide series. He is a member of the International Honor Society for Philosophy, and lives in New Haven. He is also an artist, a poet, and a hobby inventor.